Theo von Taane

Majestic Flowers
and Butterflies
Adult Coloring Book

Bibliografische Information der Deutschen Nationalbibliothek:
Die Deutsche Nationalbibliothek verzeichnet diese Publikation in der Deutschen Nationalbibliografie; detaillierte bibliografische Daten sind im Internet über http://dnb.dnb.de abrufbar.

© 2015 Theo von Taane; 1. Auflage

Text and Illustrations: **Theo von Taane**

Herstellung und Verlag: BoD – Books on Demand, Norderstedt

ISBN: 9783739227085

Contents

1. Lily
2. Bitter Root
3. Convolvulus
4. Dandelion
5. Hyacinth
6. Squill
7. Iris
8. Lilac
9. Poppy
10. Rose
11. Snowdrop
12. Tulip
13. Aquileg
14. Waterlily
15. Orchidee
16. Narcissus
17. Coneflower
18. Gaillardia
19. Cosmos
20. Dictamnus
21. Bird of paradise
22. Cyclamen
23. Rose
24. Lily
25. Nasturtium
26. Eichhorn
27. Gerbera
28. Tagetes
29. Bund of flowers 1
30. Bund of flowers 2
31. Bund of flowers 3
32. Bund of flowers 4
33. Bund of flowers 5
34. Bund of flowers 6
35. Bund of flowers 7
36. Bund of flowers 8

Books of Theo von Taane

book	ISBN / order nr.
Football note- and tactic book	9783734749605
Badminton note- and tactic book	9783734749643
Baseball note- and tactic book	9783734749650
Basketball note- and tactic book	9783734749681
Bowling note- and tactic book	9783734749698
Cricket note- and tactic book	9783734749711
Ice Hockey note- and tactic book	9783734749728
Fencing note- and tactic book	9783734749735
Field Hockey note- and tactic book	9783734749810
Football (Soccer) note- and tactic book	9783734749827
Futsal note- and tactic book	9783734749834
Handball note- and tactic book	9783734749841
Lacrosse Women note- and tactic book	9783734749858
Lacrosse Men note- and tactic book	9783734749865
Netball note- and tactic book	9783734749872
Rugby note- and tactic book	9783734749889
Chess note- and tactic book	9783734749896
Squash note- and tactic book	9783734749902
Tennis note- and tactic book	9783734749919
Table Tennis note- and tactic book	9783734749926
Volleyball note- and tactic book	9783734749933
Water Polo note- and tactic book	9783734749940